OPERATING ON THE STOCK EXCHANGE

Indispensable guide for beginners in the stock and options market

Lerbius Mark

Copyright © 2021 Lerbius Mark

All rights reserved

The characters and events portrayed in this book are fictitious. Any similarity to real persons, living or dead, is coincidental and not intended by the author.

No part of this book may be reproduced, or stored in a retrieval system, or transmitted in any form or by any means, electronic, mechanical, photocopying, recording, or otherwise, without express written permission of the publisher.

ISBN-13: 9798515890216
ISBN-10: 1477123456

Cover design by: Art Painter
Library of Congress Control Number: 2018675309
Printed in the United States of America

"The market was made to transfer money from the impatient to the patients."

WARREN BUFFETT

CONTENTS

Title Page
Copyright
Epigraph
Preface

Stock Exchange, what is this?	1
What is this Day Trade and Swing Trade guy you talk about?	3
How do I analyze stocks to find out which ones can go up or fall in price?	5
How do I invest?	7
Choosing the Broker	8
Opening the Account	9
Knowing the market environment	10
Activites I	12
Charts	13
The Candle	14
The Chart of Candles	16
Tops and Bottoms	18
Trend	19
Volatility	20
Volume	21
Support and Resistance	22

Seeing a "real" chart	24
Technical Indicators	26
Moving Averages	28
Setups or Operating Systems	30
Risk Control	31
Activities II	32
Book of Offers	33
How does the market move?	35
Buying and Selling	36
Uncovered Sale	37
Chart	38
Money vs. Stocks	39
Activities III	40
Analyzing Fundamentals	41
Type of Fundamentalist Analysis	43
Initiating analysis	44
Dividend yield	45
Price / Earnings per share	46
Equity Value of the Share	47
Price / Equity Value per Share	48
Current Liquidity	49
Ebitda	50
Net Debt / Shareholders' Equity	51
Net Debt / EBITDA	52
Net Margin	53
Return on Equity (ROE)	54
Return on Asset - ROA	55
CAGR - Compound Annual Growth Rate	56

Net Income and Net Income	57
Considerations and Summary	59
Activities IV	60
Options Market	61
What are these Options?	62
CALL Options	64
PUT Options	66
Where to see the calls and puts available?	67
In and Out of Money	71
Do not buy options. Sale!	72
An Interesting Strategy	73
Final Considerations	79

PREFACE

The purpose of this book is to prepare the reader to become a consistent and winning Trader.

You will earn money by operating Day Trade and Swing Trade without having to keep praying for the market to go your way, and you will do so using the famous options.

Be Day Trade, Be Buy and Hold, you will ALWAYS use Options!

It is not the goal to offer any fanciful millionaire method where the Trader or investor will become rich in a few weeks or earn "X reais per day".

Here the intention is that day after day he acquires guided knowledge, and in the end can obtain secure monthly income, just as the large institutions do.

These few days will save you a lot of money and will save you from unpleasant situations that you will not even know exist!

STOCK EXCHANGE, WHAT IS THIS?

The stock market is like a big trade fair. In this case the exchanges are in the form of "roles". Basically, a person will buy today a paper, say, Petrobras (or apples), for R $ 20.00, in the hope that he will go up after a few days he sells at R $ 23.00, getting 3 reais profit, or 15% profitability.

At the other end, there is the salesman. Either the seller bought the paper for R $ 19.00 and will sell you to that person for R $ 20.00 to take the profit of 1 real, or maybe this seller is speculating, making the sale for R $ 20.00 even without having the paper, thinking that the paper will fall to R $ 16.00.

Yes. Even without the part. It is as if the seller is in the overdraft, owing the broker R $ 20.00 in the hope that then the debt will fall to R $ 16.00 and he earns R $ 4.00. Most brokers allow you to use this "overdraft" (stock rental), but there are fees, obviously.

But one thing that you do not tell you is that the money, the profitability, the nectar on the stock exchange is not in the Assets, that is, in the stocks and funds. It is in derivatives, more specifically, in the options.

Options will be addressed later, but it is already worth making it clear that both assets and derivatives are important. But operating on the market without operating options is like going fishing without a boat, just sticking the rod in the sand, and waiting in the shade.

WHAT IS THIS DAY TRADE AND SWING TRADE GUY YOU TALK ABOUT?

Simple too. Day Trade is when you buy the "apple" (active) in one day, and on the same day already sells it to someone else, either by higher price (Profit) or by lower price (Loss).

Swing Trade is the name of the transaction that occurs when you buy the stock today and "secure" it, hoping to value, to sell days or months later. (Or never sell if it is a stock that pays good dividends)

One thing I can already assure the reader: Never do Day Trade. It is not profitable. It is a game.

Yes. There are thousands of Youtubers claiming to make 2% a day with Day Trade. But make a simple calculation.

Imagine that this Youtuber started with R $ 100.00 reais on 01/01/2019. In the first trading session he would have R $ 102.00. In the second trading session he would have R$ 104.04. In the third, R$ 106.12. And so, it goes.

Using compound interest, considering 20 monthly trading sessions in 24 calendar months, this Youtuber would have on 01/01/2021 a capital of R$ 1,500,000,000,000.000.00. That is, more than a trillion reais.

Comic, isn't it? Do the math there for compound interest and have a good laugh.

In addition, CVM hired FGV to conduct a survey to assess the profitability of these "Day Traders". The result was obvious. 99% of the operations were impaired. And that was not an opinion poll. The ACTUAL data **provided** for the study were used.

This youtuber who tries to trick you does not live off Day Trade. He lives on who believes in him.

The market is random. The market is manipulated in the short term, but it is not in the long run.

Final word: Follow Warren Buffet, follow Luiz Barsi, do not bet on Day Trade. Invest in Swing Trade.

Spend most of your time *studying the* market, not clicking with *your mouse* sending orders.

If you like youtubers, there are many excellent ones who are not indoctrinators of Day Trade, but rather real investors. Follow them.

HOW DO I ANALYZE STOCKS TO FIND OUT WHICH ONES CAN GO UP OR FALL IN PRICE?

There are 3 ways of analysis to try to guess the direction of the asset, whether it will fall or if it will rise from a certain moment.

Graphical analysis, also called technical analysis, relies on statistical tools, such as moving averages, to try to predict this next movement. It has existed for over a century and is widely used.

As already said, the assertiveness of technical analysis (graphic) increases as we look more in the long term, after all, it is statistics.

There is also fundamentalist analysis, which uses as parameters the business data of the company itself. That is, the fundamentals analyst will check the company's profit in the last quarter, its debt, if it pays dividends, if the price is far above the total equity of the company, among other fundamentalist indicators.

Finally, there is flow analysis. It was widely used in the era of paper trading and was called Tape Reading. Today it still exists and is used, but as the market is basically operationalized by robots, its manual use is unfeasible.

And worse, today assets have a lot of volatility (rapid price variation). In the old days, the assets had small variation from one day to the next. It was easier to perform this analysis.

But it is still widely used.

You must choose 2 of these shapes. You cannot operate with just one of them.

In this book, we will use fundamentalist analysis and graphic analysis.

HOW DO I INVEST?

To make an investment, there are dozens of banks and brokers that provide the service and platforms for operation. Some charging brokerages and some not.

Right away, I suggest running away from big banks. They charge dearly and do not offer proper platforms or Home Brokers.

But that's obvious, the big bank profits from selling you CBD, profiting from your money sat on savings. In the stock market he does not make a profit.

So, on this first day, we are going to open an account at a brokerage firm. No fees!

It does not matter if you own too much or too little money, if you are reading this chapter, you will not start small. You are going to learn. Have low risk. That is how it works healthily.

Opening an account at the broker is simpler than you might think. It is much faster than opening the account at a bank. In less than 24 hours your account is approved, and you can already make transfers.

CHOOSING THE BROKER

The broker to be chosen does not need to have zero brokerage fee. It just needs to be cheap.

Why is that? Because you are not a Day Trader. You will perform few operations.

But of course, if we have good options for zero-rate brokers, we are going to choose them.

There is no partnership with broker, you choose the one that feels best.

In United States, use TD Ameritrade. Free Comission and has the best platform.

So, it is my indication to start in the world of the stock market. Start. One step at a time.

OPENING THE ACCOUNT

It is extremely simple to open an account at Td Ameritrade. Just click on the suggestive Open your Account. Enter all the data and wait in your email for confirmation.

Do it now. Search Google for Td Ameritrade and open your account.

There is no secret. It is quite simple indeed.

We will get back to it later.

Yes. Later. Because in next pages you will learn to read graphics, and after it you will learn to analyze companies by the fundamentals.

You did not think you would go out and operate on the brokerage without knowing how to do that, did you?

Remember the issue of anxiety.

KNOWING THE MARKET ENVIRONMENT

The market environment is not just your broker's website. Everything messes with the market.

Therefore, we need to outsource certain information, using some free services available.

One of them I recommend (not only me but most investors) is the Investing.Com website.

It is fantastic for graphic analysis, and to even control your portfolio and still have access to market news, the suggestion is the investing.com.

The site, also completely free, has advanced tools for technical/graphic analysis, and is widely used by traders.

Of course if you open a Td Ameritrade account the Think or Swim Platform will give you completely everything you need.

But, if you choose another brookerage, use the website.

Rest assured, as early as next day you will learn to read this chart easily.

Explore this site a lot.

ACTIVITES I

We conclude this first day of learning by presenting the best tools for your analysis and creating your account at the most suitable broker for beginners.

Now, as an exercise, explore the two sites presented and wait for your account to be approved at the broker.

We are going to have a task.

2) Open the site investing.com and create an account.

    Select your language. Read the news and turn on notifications. Then we will go deeper.

Rest.

CHARTS

There are several types of charts on the market, but here because it is dynamic, we will be practical and guide to what most traders use. The chart of candles, or Candle Stick.

The chart is a tool for use in graphical analysis. Shows the price history. It is possible to operate the market without using the chart, but as stated before, we will act with technical analysis and fundamentalist analysis.

THE CANDLE

The candle chart consists of: Candles!

It is called candles by their appearance because it has wicks (the traces above or below the candles).

See below the bullish candle (green). There opening indicates the first trading price. Closing indicates the last trading price. The y-coordinate, vertical, is the price.

Therefore, it is very suggestive that the closure is above the opening. Clear. It opened for example at R$ 10.00 and closed the R$ 12.00. The bearish candle, the other way around.

And what are wicks? The wicks are times when the price came to go there but returned and closed at another point. The minimum and the maximum.

It is possible a Candle without any wick, or without only 1 of the wicks. It is sufficient that the closing and/or opening coincide so low or maximum.

OPERATING ON THE STOCK EXCHANGE

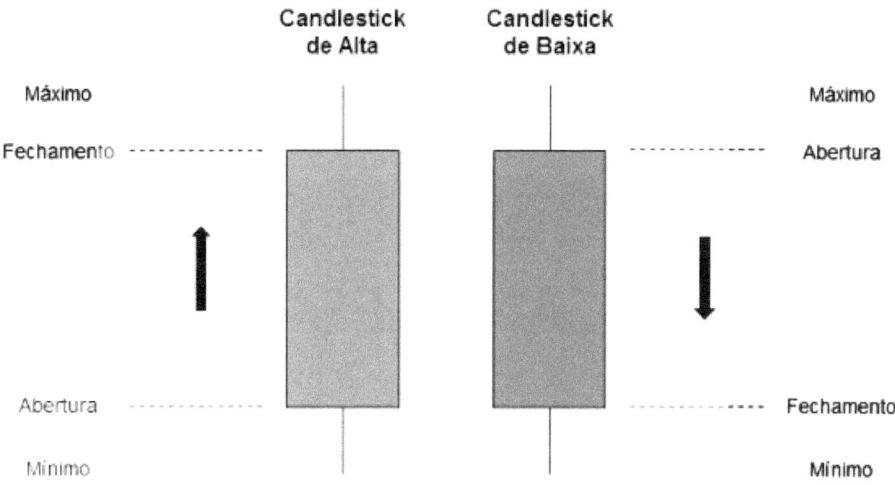

THE CHART OF CANDLES

The candle chart, as the name says, is a set of candles that represent the past of the asset's price change. See below how easy it is for us to identify the breadth of price movement for a stock by looking at the candle chart.

Important information about the chart above is to talk about time frame, or time chart.

It basically means how long it takes to form each candle on the chart.

For example, in daily time, each candle is equivalent to 1 trading day.

In the 60-minute time chart, each candle indicates 1 hour of price

change.
After 60 minutes, a new Candle opens.

TOPS AND BOTTOMS

The chart routinely generates tops and bottoms. They are important in technical analysis because prices have failed to pass from there and have gone back in the opposite direction.

TOPO

FUNDO

The importance is the memory of prices. If the last time you went up, no one wanted to buy above $ 14.95, I will try to sell the $ 15.00? Of course, I am not. I have seen it before!

TREND

In the previous figure you noticed that from the top the asset hitched a sequence of falls. We call it a Downtrend.

On the contrary, we can also have the Uptrend after a fund.

Note that even in the downtrend, there are times when the asset has increased, that is, it has had positive (green) candles. This is precisely because of the "breaths" of the market.

These vents are usually by investors who are making their profits, that is, terminating their operations with "gain", because they fear that the asset may reverse the trend soon.

In time, it is also possible for an asset not to be in any defined trend, which we call consolidation. It is when the asset is only varying between a certain price range, without going through it neither up nor down.

VOLATILITY

Volatility is represented by asset price changes in a short time, without affecting its current trend.

We call it high volatility the fact that the price of the asset goes up orca go fast.

There are traders who exploit volatility, and there are traders who exploit the trend.

VOLUME

Volume is the measure of the number of trades executed on a given candle, or the financial value of those trades.

It is especially useful to check whether that candle is relevant or not.

Candles with low volume are usually just "vents" of the market.

On the other, candles with high volumes usually indicate a trend that may be confirmed.

SUPPORT AND RESISTANCE

We call support the price zone in which the asset when falling, usually does not pass it.

For example, if we saw that T (AT&T) fell to 31.00 for 3 times and did not go down, we have set up a support there.

That does not mean the price is not going to go down below that. It is just an interesting zone for you to "bet" on the rise of the asset, that is, on the reversal of the current trend.

Above we can visually see the support and resistance plotted on the chart.

Note that it is not a certainty that the price will not cross these levels. There is only a greater chance that it will not go from there. It is certainly a particularly useful tool to be plotted on the chart.

SEEING A "REAL" CHART

Now let us do an exercise. Open the investing.com.

Click on the top of the flag to select the one from your country. I will use Brazillian stocks in examples.

Important: Stock Market is basically the same in all the world. Candle charts are EXACTLY the same.

Then in the search field on the site, type PETR4 and select it to appear the Asset information.

Then look for the "Technical Chart" option and click the icon to expand in full screen.

When you open the chart, click the Candlestick icon to turn the chart into a candlestick chart, as shown in the image below.

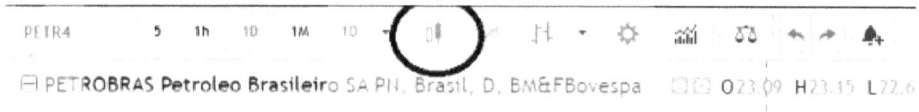

Now your chart is like Candlestick.

Note the selected Time Frame. It is in 1D in the image above, i.e., each candle represents 1 trading day. You can change to 5 (minutes), 1 hour, 1 month etc. For now, we will operate only in 1D, also called the daily chart.

Hold control and use the mouse scroll (middle button) to zoom in and out.

Try viewing brackets and resistances, tops, and bottoms, which have occurred in the last 2 months of trading. Also try to observe the trend.

Also note the volume bars below the chart.

There is no right or wrong right now. It is just his first critical view of a candlestick chart. He will be part of your life from today.

TECHNICAL INDICATORS

The chart allows the use of so-called Technical Indicators.

They are divided into volatility indicators (detect likely short-term changes), and trend indicators (detect changes in the current trend, from up to low and from low to high.)

There are thousands of indicators in the world, and many of them are redundant.

Since here is not a specific book of technical analysis, I will present only the indicator called RSI - Relative Strength Index.

Many investors use only this indicator in their analyses, leaving the rest for fundamentalist analysis, and for Price Action (analyze price x volume x support and resistance).

Let us see in practice how it works.

Reopen the site investing.com and start a technical graph of PETR4.

Switch to Candles chart as it was done in the previous topic. Leave the time chart in 1D - Daily.

Then click the button indicated below, called Indicators/Slash, or Indicators.

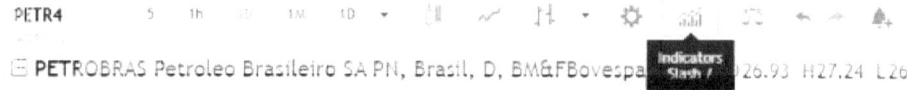

Select the RSI indicator - Relative Strength Index. It will appear below the candle chart.

The default setting for this indicator is 14 periods. Leave it at that.

A quick explanation: This indicator assesses price strength. When the RSI is above 70, usually this indicates that there is a high chance that the price will start a fall. This is because there is indication that there was an exaggerated "stretched" without rest.

It is as if the market is excited about the asset, all buying, but by reaching 70 or more, these investors are already starting to sell, to make profit.

When the RSI reaches a level of 30 down, it is an indication that the price can rise. There was an excess of sales (market oversold) and so there is expectation that the purchases will return.

Look, it is an expectation. Technical analysis is not a logical science. It is statistical. It uses probabilities. But certainly, when an asset has IFR in '90, it can be a bad time to buy it.

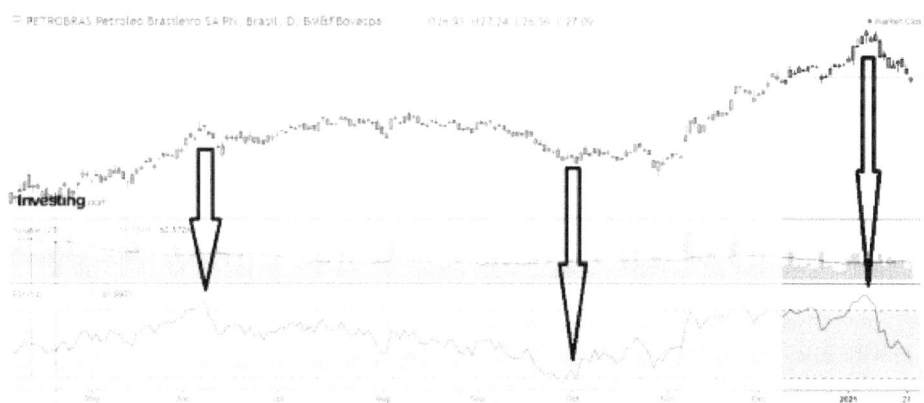

As said, there are thousands of indicators.

But I believe that to start in the market, it is enough to work only with Price, Volume, RSI and Moving Averages, which we will see in the next chapter.

MOVING AVERAGES

Moving averages are of utmost importance in a chart. First because with them you can notice the short- or long-term trend.

In addition, institutional investors use averages to enter and exit operations.

In fact, moving averages are kind of an indicator. But here we treat it as an autonomous tool for didactic purposes only.

The moving average is an average that walks with time.

For example, you want to view the 3-day moving average. That is, 3 periods. This means that everything that happened before that will not enter the calculation of the average.

Let us say today is Thursday. The 3-day moving average will be: (Tuesday Price + Wednesday Price + Thursday Price) / 3.

When a day passes, and we arrive on Friday, the 3-day moving average will be calculated as well:

(Wednesday Price + Thursday Price + Friday Price) / 3.

That is the arithmetic moving average.

But what if the data of the nearest day is more important than the data of the farthest day? That is, what if in the last example I wanted the Sixth to have more weight than Wednesday?

For this, the Exponential moving average was created. It gives more weight to the latest data.

Now, let us get to practice.

Open the investing.com, go to the indicators area, and select Moving Average or the Moving Average Exponential. (Arithmetic Moving Average or Exponential Moving Average)

⊟ PETROBRAS Petroleo Brasileiro SA PN, Brasil, D, BM&FBovespa
MA (9, close, 0)   22.8362

The average chart will be plotted on the chart, which acts as a guide. This above is the average of 9 arithmetic periods. Each investor selects the period that best suits their market view.

The average of 9 periods indicates the short-term trend, and the average of 200 periods signals to us the long-term trend.

There are authors who indicate the use of the Moving Average of 21 periods as the average of the institutional, that is, the players who move the stock exchange in swing trade.

SETUPS OR OPERATING SYSTEMS

The famous term Setup indicates a repetitive sequence of operations, some with profit and others at a loss, so that on the whole you win since the winning operations generate(theoretically) more money than the losing operations.

In this book you will not learn how to use Setups simply because they are just another way to use the financial market as a betting game and not a chess game.

An example of Setup is that of RSI Whenever the asset reaches RSI at 30 you will buy it, and whenever the asset reaches at 70 you will sell it. Setup does not analyze macroeconomics, nor nearby events, nor volume, anything. In that case it would be like a robot operating.

It is a way the anxious have found themselves to discipline themselves. It is still a valid technique. But it is not the one that is going to give you a long life in the market.

RISK CONTROL

Risk control is used by Traders to minimize their loss when applying on the stock exchange. In these 5 days you will learn how to do risk control with options.

There are other methods like "Stop Loss Order", that is, you set the maximum loss you want. It is widely used by speculators. Nothing nice to define your injury, is it?

I am not saying she is wrong. After all, the market is random. The speculator's betting. Even more day traders and those who use Setups.

But as already pointed out by many studies, the bettor Day Trader has a short life. The use of Stop only allows it to suffer more time on the market. Without Stop Loss, his death would be swift. And no addict wants to overdose. They want to die slowly and enjoying the illusion of winning and lose.

But you will not be a mere speculator. You will be an investor with knowledge of options. You will not invest seeking 2% per day. There is no such thing. No insider.

ACTIVITIES II

Finally, we will follow the progress of a chart during the trading session using the Investing.com.

Open the investing.com at trading time and choose an asset by opening its chart and stir in the timesheet (periodicity), place averages and indicators.

See how prices move. As the candles and wicks form during the day.

Of course, if your Think or Swim platform is already fired, use it !

BOOK OF OFFERS

The order book is where the purchase and sale offer of a particular asset are recorded.

In Think or Swim, we have:

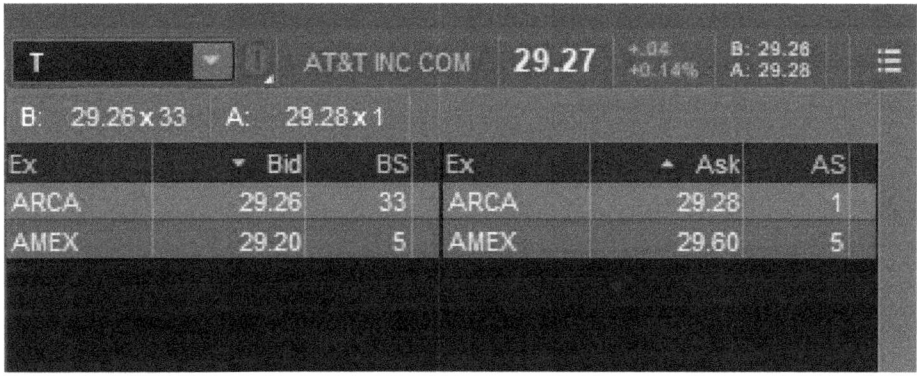

See above a book of offers in practice. Ex means Exchange. B is BID and A is ASK. Bid is the column where people are giving money (bidding) and ask is the column where people are asking for money (selling stock).

In the example above, there are 33 orders wanting to buy 1 T at R$ 29.26 and there is only 1 order wanting to sell at R$ 29.28.

Important: Your order only goes to the book if it is of the limited type.

If you want to buy the market, you will automatically pay the cheapest price that sellers are offering, and in the case of the image above is $ 29.28. That is why the market order does not go to the book. Because it is instant. It alters the book.

So why up there indicates that the last price is $ 29.27?

Simple. Because the price of the asset is the last traded price. That is, the last transaction was at this value.

HOW DOES THE MARKET MOVE?

Look again at the picture of the Book of Offerings.

Notice that what moves the market are the market orders! Because the book is just a bunch of deals where sellers want to sell expensive and buyers want to buy cheap, in their view.

When someone is thinking that the asset will rise, sends an order to the market.

When someone thinks the asset will fall, it sends a sale to the market.

The name of that is "Aggression." Assault of Purchase and Assault of Sale. Without aggression, the market would not be a Trading Session but an eternal Auction.

BUYING AND SELLING

After your analysis, let us say you have defined that you want to buy the T asset on the market, because the currently traded price is already low according to its interpretation. It satisfies you.

You send an order to the market and you will buy the asset, say, for $25.40 each share.

You are then "positioned" in the asset in a purchased operation.

Let us say that the asset 3 days later is quoted at R$ 29.00 and that you for some reason no longer want to be positioned in this company.

In this case you send a sales order. It can be the market, that is, R$ 29.00 that is the current price (changes every second), or it can be a limited sales order, for say R$ 35.00.

If the asset reaches R$ 35.00, it will be sold. If you do not, it will not be.

The important thing is that you will earn the profit from the operation. Sale price minus purchase price.

UNCOVERED SALE

This is the situation where you do not have the asset in your wallet, but you think the price of it will drop and you want to speculate to gain from the drop.

For this, you will do an uncovered salve. Will sell something you do not have.

In this case, you will sell the paper for example at R$ 35.00 and rebuy it says at R$ 24.00.

You will pay a rental fee for it.

Rent, because you will rent someone's asset at the "Rental Bank".

Yes. You can also offer your assets in portfolio for rent. And you are going to get paid for it.

But do not worry about it now. We will not address this in this initial book.

Just know that it is possible to operate sold, that is, without owning the asset. And this is done on a large scale in the market.

CHART

Now click on Chart in your Think or Swim or open investing.com website and click in charts:

Then appears the chart of Candles, which you already know. It is the same as there is investing.com but here in real time. Back in Investing.com he has a 15-minute delay.

You can include Studies (indicators), you can include Drawings (for example, using a horizontal line to mark a resistance or a support.

MONEY VS. STOCKS

Yes. You need to have money in the broker's account to operate.

You can transfer to the and the money comes in quickly.

Transactions are not settled instantly, but this is an operational issue.

For you, investor, it is as if buying the money immediately went to the seller, and when selling, you get the money also instantly.

But the money is not available for cash. It takes two days for that. What happens is the fact that the broker gives you the "credit" of this money for you to buy more shares.

That is, if you have an asset say XOM, and sold the lot for $ 500.00, immediately you will have in your account $ 500.00 available to buy other shares. But only in 2 days you can withdraw these R $ 500.00 to your bank account. That is what I am saying.

ACTIVITIES III

Explore the other functions of Home Broker.

Today you should spend the day watching the papers move. See how the roles behave, how the moving averages are forming, that is, to settle with the market.

Remember to always keep open a financial news site like the investing.com or another of your choice. I point out investing.com it is free and quality.

But remember, you cannot have anxious mind, i.e., day trader mind.

You will always operate to buy in a day and sell days later, or even months later.

So, if you want to simulate operations, simulate for example a point where you would buy today, and tomorrow, see what your operation would look like.

Look, just simulate. With a piece of paper. Write down the price you thought would be the minimum today. You will see it is impossible to do that. It is a long shot. The market is unpredictable.

But with graphical analysis, supports, resistances, you can improve your hit to up to 60%.

ANALYZING FUNDAMENTALS

Fundamentalist Indicators

Okay, now you know how to buy stocks and already know how to analyze charts.

We now need to learn how to analyze the fundamentals of the company, that is, we need to know if the company is good or not. If it is worth investing in.

But what if I just want to speculate, not invest?

Even so you need to know the size of the hole in which you are including yourself.

Here our focus is investment, but in any case, you cannot treat the paper as just a Ticker (code) like T or MSFT. You need to analyze it in full.

For this, we have fundamentalist indicators.

As already handled, this book is practical. So, we will not dwell on talking about the theories of indicators, nor will we go out explaining them all.

You will learn how to do the analysis, and we will do this by taking the information from some website, such as Status Invest, which is free.

This analysis usually will do 1 time per quarter. In fact, you do the first full analysis and get to know the asset.

Subsequently, every 3 months the company's quarterly results are disclosed and then it is necessary to accompany it to see if things are going in the right direction.

TYPE OF FUNDAMENTALIST ANALYSIS

Just to register, there are several types of analysis, such as macroeconomics (global economy and its links), qualitative analysis (sector of activity, ability of managers), quantitative (by company results), and valuation (where it seeks to calculate the fair price of the share).

Here in this book, because it is focused on beginners, we will address quantitative analysis, focused on the results that the company presents quarterly.

INITIATING ANALYSIS

By opening the Think or Swim, we type above the ticker of the asset, for example, AR, we will have the fundamentalist indicators already calculated for us.

In the past, there were no such tools. The analysts did the calculations in hand, and only after years of courses.

Now, in a few days you already become a beginner stock analyst without having to calculate such elements.

DIVIDEND YIELD

The famous DY (Dividend Yield) is the percentage of earnings in dividends that the stock has generated in the last 12 months, considering its current quote.

So, let us say EOLS is quoted at R$ 20.00 and has dividend yield of 10%.

This indicates that in the last 12 months, it has delivered $ 2.00 of dividend to shareholders.

That is, by dividing this value by 12, we have a monthly income of 0.83% on top of the amount invested.

But a market maxim must be repeated: Past yields are not collateral for future yields.

Therefore, the correct thing is that you analyze your asset continuously. Quarterly.

At the end of today you will learn a basic way to predict the dividend that will be delivered in the future. No complications or exorbitant calculations.

PRICE / EARNINGS PER SHARE

Especially important indicator is the price under earnings per share (divided by earnings per share).

It is the value that as wells whether investors are optimistic or not about the company's profit in the future. If the value is too high, they may be optimistic, or perhaps the share price is too expensive. (over-optimism)

On the contrary, too. If the value is low, or the market is selling cheap the asset, or the market thinks that past profits will not be repeated but reduced.

The calculation is simple. Considering the current price (R$ 20.00) divided by Annual Earnings per share (R$ 2,000,000.00 divided by the 500,000 papers in the market, it generates an LPA of R$ 4.00for each paper.

Picking up then 20.00/4 we have a hypothetical PL above 5.

Therefore, investing 20.00 reais in the company, it will take 5 years to recover the money invested, based on the profits that the company has today.

We also say that this company today works with multiple profits in 5x.

Ideal is to compare companies from the same sector with this indicator, to choose for example which of the bank papers you will or will not invest.

EQUITY VALUE OF THE SHARE

It is also a simple calculation indicator.

It is the total equity of the company divided by the number of shares issued.

It is as if it were what equity value in reais that each share has.

So, if calculating resulted for example in R $ 12.00 and the stock today is priced at R $ 13.00, indicates that it is valued. Which is worth more than your assets.

It should never be analyzed in isolation because there are companies that do not have equity, and there are others that "inflate" equity with intangible assets, such as expectation of future profits after a certain business expansion.

PRICE / EQUITY VALUE PER SHARE

Also, a useful indicator and simple calculation. You take the current price and divide by the equity value of the share, explained above.

With that, we will have a multiple. If this multiple is below 1, and it is not a period of crisis in the market, we have that the company is in serious trouble and it is not recommended to invest in it, even if it is cheap.

However, if it is a time of crisis, it is possible that the market is just afraid and that it is a good opportunity.

An exceedingly high number can make it difficult to value the company, because it is already well above its price. At the same time, it can be a solid company, good dividend payer, and that will not give you a headache in the future.

CURRENT LIQUIDITY

Current liquidity is an easy-to-see indicator. It is the company's ability to pay in the short term. It is like a checking account balance for use. It is the division between current assets and current liabilities.

The ideal is a value above 1, that is, more current assets than current liabilities.

Values below 1 indicate the company's difficulty in the short term and turn on the warning signal.

EBITDA

Ebitda is Earnings before interest, taxes, depreciation and amortization.

It is useful for buying business between different countries because it does not include taxes in your calculation.

It also excludes depreciation, and this is quite interesting because the calculation of depreciation of goods is not the same from one country to another.

There is also adjusted EBITDA, which excludes non-recurring facts, i.e., a fine for example.

There is also EBIT, which is profit before interest and taxes. That is, it includes depreciation and amortization in the calculation. But we will not use it in this basic book.

NET DEBT / SHAREHOLDERS' EQUITY

Basically, it is the total debt divided by total assets and rights.

The ideal is to locate companies that have this indicator below 0.5, that is, below 50%.

If a company has more debt than its Net Worth, that is, indicator above 1, or 100%, is a bad indicator. The company is heavily indebted.

NET DEBT / EBITDA

Next, you should analyze the Net Debt/EBITDA indicator. It indicates the level of debt and how much the company currently generates from its operational activities.

The amount is the number of years that the company would take to pay the entire debt, considering its results.

Ebitda is Earnings Before Interest, Taxes, Depreciation and Amortization.

Whether the company will take 4 or 5 years to pay off all its debt based on EBITDA is a negative indicator, denoting difficulties for the company.

Ideally, the value of 2 for this indicator, or less.

One note: This indicator may appear negative. This is because the company's EBITDA may be negative, accumulating losses, which is even worse.

NET MARGIN

Net margin is an indicator of efficiency.

It is what percentage of the total revenue of the company that has effectively become profit.

It is Net Income/Net Revenue.

It should be analyzed together, after all, a company that has a high net margin but owns Net Debt/EBITDA above 5 indicates that the company is profitable, but billing is extremely low near its total debt.

In the case above, the analyst should be very attentive because any fall in the margin would represent a chaotic situation of a price-less debt.

Or the company would make new loans to pay off the current debt until one day it can no longer borrow and become insolvent.

RETURN ON EQUITY (ROE)

The ROE, or Return on Equity, indicates how much the company can generate from profit without needing other companies, that is, using its equity.

It is the division between Net Income / Equity.

It is possibly the most important indicator of analysts. A high ROE indicates a company with good administration.

However, it is necessary to verify the level of indebtedness of the company, as this may compromise the analysis.

A company with high debt to be won in the coming quarters may have its ROE significantly affected when it must honor that commitment because its net profit will fall.

The ROE should be compared between companies in the same sector because there are sectors in which companies do not have high net worth, such as the service sector.

A 10% ROE in the banking sector for example is considered very satisfactory, although historically the sector has reached about 25% ROE.

RETURN ON ASSET - ROA

The ROA (Return on Assets) indicates the company's profitability in relation to its assets (assets, credits, and rights).

That is, it is the return on the effective equity of the company, unlike the ROE, which inequity, which may include the intangible assets.

Care is needed for the intangible because it is an expectation. For example, if a company buys a brand, that brand will be an intangible asset and may have a high value that in the future may not represent all that capital that has-been imagined.

CAGR - COMPOUND ANNUAL GROWTH RATE

The CAGR - Compound Annual Growth Rate - is an indicator that can be calculated considering the Profits or considering the Revenue.

For example, we have 2 companies A and B.

Investing R$ 10,000.00 in company A and R$ 10,000.00 in company B for 5 years.

If we consider that in this period company A had cagr approximately 1% and company B had CAGR of 9% our capital of R$ 10,0000.00 would have become approximately R$ 10,500.00 in company A and approximately 15,300.00% in company B.

The focus here is not the calculation or the formula. It is to show the effect of CAGR in abstract.

The formula is CAGR = (End Value / Starting Value)$^{1/N}$ - 1, where N is how many years have passed.

But watch out. The CAGR ignores the oscillations within this period. Therefore, it needs to be calculated at least at 5 years, and be aware that it is a long-term indicator.

NET INCOME AND NET INCOME

Net revenue is the amount that the company has increased from sales, discounting the costs they generate by itself, as taxes (under the products), chargebacks, among others.

Net income is net revenue debilled from all other company expenses.

Let us look at a diagram of the Status Invest website:

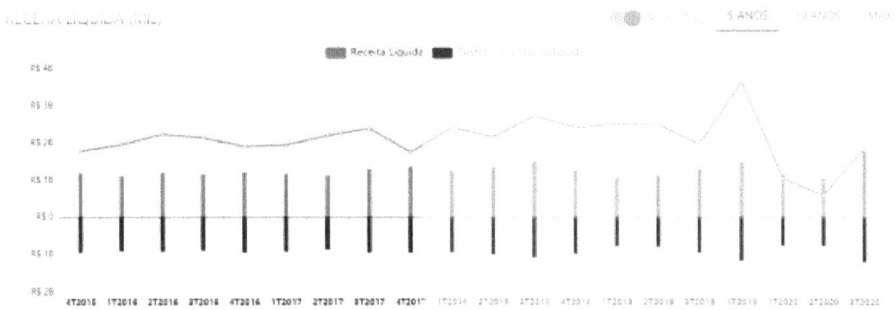

See how easy the tool is to see. When we select the Quarterly option, we have the graph of net income bringing us that this company reduced its net revenue in 1Q20 and 2Q20 (coronavirus pandemic), but also reduced its costs, demonstrating that there is good management. In 3Q20 we see a recovery in net income.

It is always important to remember that net income can include non-recurring facts, such as the sale of a building by a construction company.

Therefore, one should pay little to the niche market that is being analyzed.

CONSIDERATIONS AND SUMMARY

There are several professional ways to perform a fundamental analysis.

Here is a practical manual for the beginner. It makes no sense to go into metrics such as discounted cash flow, among other tools used to measure the fair price of a stock.

The idea is that at the end of reading you can invest with awareness.

Of course, over time, you will continue studying and perfecting your skills.

ACTIVITIES IV

You performed your first fundamentalist analysis successfully.

Of course, a graduate analyst from a large institution will lean hedling a lot on companies to squeeze the data and try to pursue a positive or negative bias, based on the positioning of their employer.

In addition, the task of analyzing the company cannot be extremely exhausting, otherwise you alone will never be able to analyze many companies and with that, will not find good opportunities.

Finally, I record that the analysis should be yours. Never accept analyses from others without checking if there is sense in what has been said. And now you already have minimal knowledge for it.

Time and reading will perfect it.

An important task to be done is to register your email in all IR (Investor Relations) of the companies you are accompanying and want to be a partner.

This will allow you to be informed firsthand.

To do this, go on google, enter the company ticker and on the RI front.
For example, "MSFT IR"

The first result will usually be where you will register your email.

Search for Mailing or something, and register.

OPTIONS MARKET

Now let us go to the nectar of operations in the financial market.

This is where the winners are hiding.

Or not so hidden, since in the U.S. for example in 2019 were operated 20 million contracts of options per day.

WHAT ARE THESE OPTIONS?

Options are instruments that you can trade in your broker, as well as stocks, real estate funds, among others.

Each option also has a Ticker (code), for example, MSFT is the asset and .MSFT210618P80 is the option.

Then, the option appears on the chart, has volume, price, that is, you operate it in the very same way that operates a normal asset. We got off to a good start.

And what are the differences then? Option of what? Why that confusing name?

Come on, let us go, let us.

There are two kinds of options. CALLS and PUTS. (I will use the universal term to facilitate here).

For example, .MSFT210618C80 is a CALL and .MSFT210618P80 is an example of PUT, both correlated with the asset MSFT.

Every option is derived from some asset. That is why we call derivatives options.

Now, see the ticker: .MSFT210618C80.

It means: 210618 is the last date the option will have life. 21 is the year of 2021. 06 is for june and 18 is the day.

next we have C80.

C is for CALL and P is for PUT.

80 is the Strike price of the option.

So the ticker of an option is always coded using the underlying stock ticker, the year with 2 digits, the month, the day with 2 digits, the letter C or P and the strike price.

CALL OPTIONS

Right. I have options that are CALL type and I have put options. That is two kinds of options. OK.

Every option, whether call or put, has the following most basic parameters: Strike Price (also called strike price) and Strike Date.

First let us go with the CALLs. If you buy a call, for example, you bought 100 calls from T, for example.

This call has strike price (Strike) let us say 23,90 and due on 02/22/2021.

What does that mean? It means that the holder of this call (i.e., who is bought on the call), has the right to say: I want to buy T (the stock, underlying) at 23.90. This is exercising the CALL option.

Call gives the holder the power to require that the player who sold him the call has an obligation to sell him the correlated asset (in this case T) at the strike price (exercise).

And if the asset is worth 30.00, the call holder can force the launcher to sell his T for only 23.90? Yes! That is the essence of it.

Who buys a call and chooses the strike for example 18.00 is betting that the asset will rise above 18.00 and with that after the asset is say there at 24.00, he will exercise the call, that is, the pitcher (who sold him the call, who closed the "contract" with him) will have to sell to him the T at the price of 18.00?

What if T is 15.00? In that case the call holder will not want to exercise, because if he exercises, he will buy at 18.00 which does not make sense since on the market today he would buy at 15.00, cheaper.

The option is called option because whoever buys it will have an "option" to choose whether to exercise your option!

Calls are the Purchase options. It gives the right indicated above. Buy the asset of the one who launched.

What about the launcher? What is in it for you?

Simple. The launcher sold the call. This sale costs money like any other trade. This money that the holder paid him to have the call is called "prize".

If you arrive on 22/02, the day of maturity, and the holder does not exercise the CALL, that is, do not exercise the option to purchase the asset, then the option "turns to dust". It is no longer negotiated. And the option disappears. In this case the launcher "got a prize".

What if the holder (who bought the call) exercises the option to buy? As already said, it will force the pitcher (who sold the option to buy him) to deliver (sell) T at the strike price. The clear launcher will keep the award it has already received, and will also receive the amount related to T, which will be sold to the holder in the price of striking.

PUT OPTIONS

In the same way that we have the CALLS, purchase options, we have the PUTs, which are the selling options.

The idea is the same. However, it is not the right to require the asset to be purchased, as in calls. Here the right is to sell. Put is a selling option. The holder has the right to exercise the option and sell the asset to the launcher. If this happens, the pitcher is required to purchase it at the strike price.

Similarly, the put has a strike and a due date.

After expiration, if the holder does not exercise the PUT (the option to sell), then it turns to dust.

WHERE TO SEE THE CALLS AND PUTS AVAILABLE?

Fire your prefered platform. I will use a service just to demonstrate that the essence of options is the same in all the world. I will use brazillian Petrobrás. PETR4 in brazillian stock market. PBR in Dow Jones.

If you are using Think or Swim, fire it and go to Trade tab.

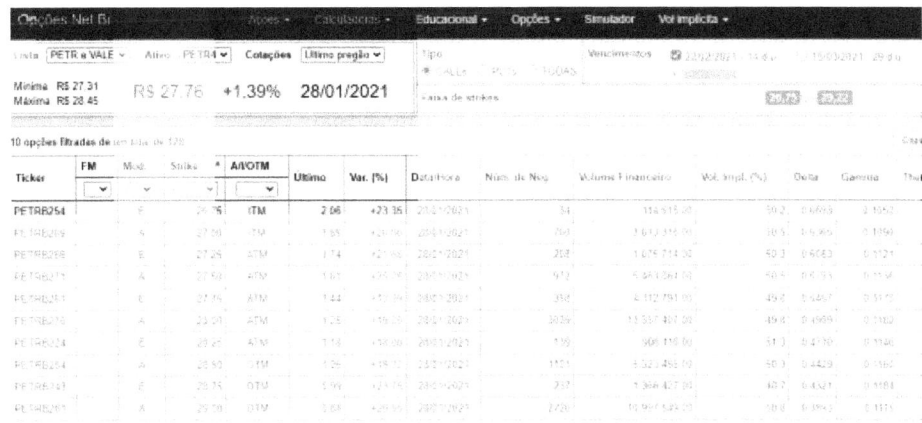

Let us just get to Strike and pay for now.

See in the table that the call PETRB284 has strike R $ 28,50 and winning 22/02/2021, and that today it is costing R $ 1,05.

The asset today is quoted at R$ 27.76. Then, whoever buys the CALL will "hope" that the asset reaches the strike value by 22/02. So, it will be worth exercising the option.

After all, if PETR4 is more front quoted at R $ 30.00 for example, he can require the launcher that sells to him at R $ 28.50. Nice deal. He can then go to the market and sell for R $ 30.00 if you want.

Let us look at the chart to improve the visualization.

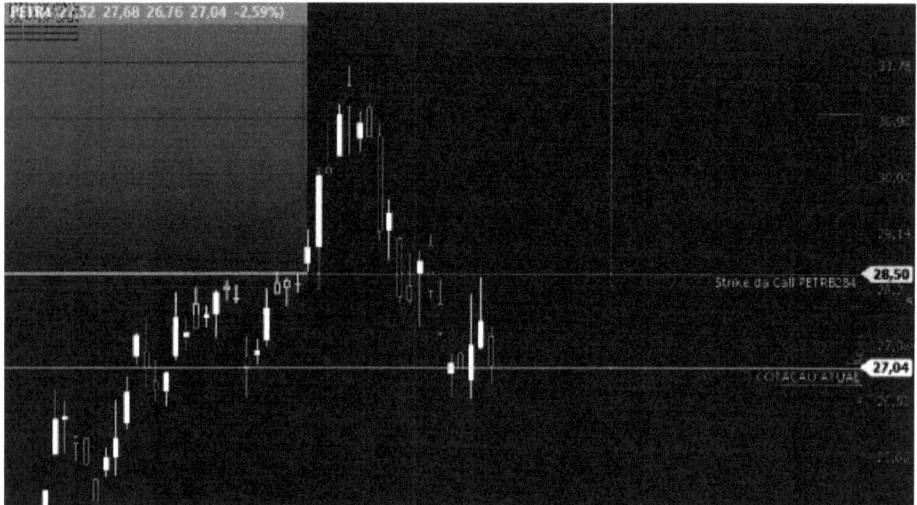

See the chart above. The move that the buyer of CALL expects is that of the rise of the asset.

The seller of CALL expects a fall in the price of the asset.

On the same site we can also see the PUTS:

Ticker	FM	Mod.	Strike	A/I/OTM	Último	Var. (%)	Data/Hora	Núm. de Neg.	Volume Financeiro	Vol. Impl. (%)	Delta
PETRN254		E	26.75	OTM	0.85	-22.43	28/01/2021	217	1.147.710,00	51.1	-0.3368
PETRN269	✓	E	27.00	OTM	0.95	-20.83	28/01/2021	3884	17.973.190,00	49.1	0.3815
PETRN266		E	27.25	ATM	1.02	-29.31	28/01/2021	271	1.467.601,00	49.8	-0.3956
PETRN271		E	27.50	ATM	1.10	-24.14	28/01/2021	553	2.983.893,00	49.9	-0.4149
PETRN261		E	27.75	ATM	1.22	-22.78	28/01/2021	222	1.004.438,00	48.6	-0.4461
PETRN276	✓	E	28.00	ATM	1.43	-18.76	28/01/2021	1450	7.616.108,00	48.9	-0.5011
PETRN224		E	28.25	ATM	1.47	-20.54	28/01/2021	45	264.710,00	45.0	-0.5066
PETRN284		E	28.50	ITM	1.65	-18.83	28/01/2021	183	557.409,00	47.4	-0.5633
PETRN243		E	28.75	ITM	1.79	-8.77	28/01/2021	185	403.296,00	49.0	-0.5738
PETRN281	✓	E	29.00	ITM	1.92	-20.00	28/01/2021	421	6.827.105,00	48.8	-0.5948

See that PUTS have the same parameters as CALLs. Again, let us just get to the winning and the strike.

PUT PETRN254 has strike R $ 26.75 and winning 22/02.

So, whoever buys this PUT is rooting for the asset to drop in price until it reaches at least its strike or preferably fall further. So, he can exercise the PUT (put option) and thus sell his PETR4 to the holder at the higher price than will be on the market, that is, sells for R $ 26.75.

What about the launcher? The pitcher twists that the asset does not reach the strike price. Is that it? The option turns to dust and the launcher gets the prize he has already received when selling the option, as it happens in CALLS.

In the chart below we see more clearly the scenario.

The asset is at that current delimited quote, while the PUT strike is below it.

The PUT buyer is waiting for the asset to fall, and the PUT seller does not want this. For the launcher, the asset does not even have to go up. Just do not fall below the strike.

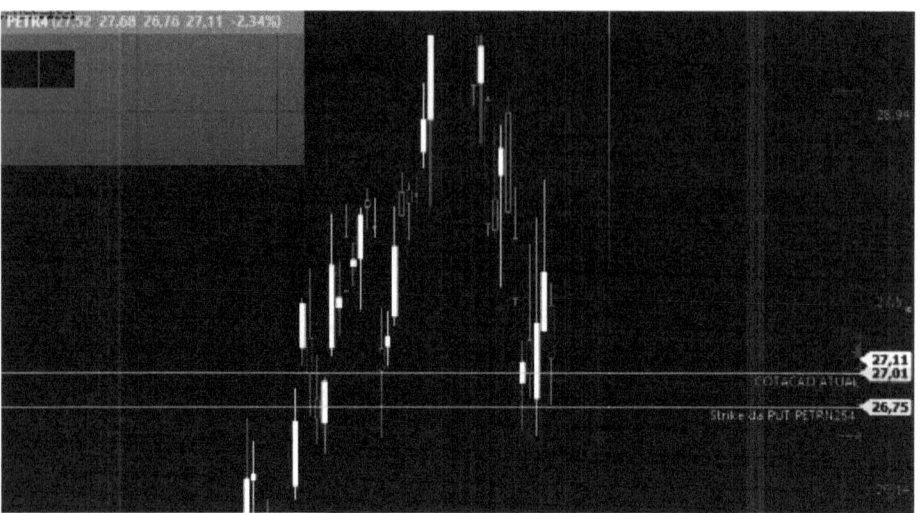

IN AND OUT OF MONEY

There are three "positions" in which the strike of the option can be in relation to the correlated asset.

If the CALL strike is far above the current price, we say it is Out of The Money, or OTM – Out of the Money.
An option out of money has, now, little chance of being exercised. That is why it is called Out of Money.

If you are close to the point where we cannot define whether it will be exercised, i.e., the price of the asset is close to the strike price, we say that the option is No Money or ATM – At the Money.

If the asset price is trading above the CALL strike or below the PUT strike, we say that this option is Inside Cash, ITM, In the Money. That is, I can buy the option now and already exercise it because the price of it is already favorable in relation to Strike. It is a No Money option. ITM.

Buying a CALL or PUT that is OTM is always cheaper, as buyers have little interest in an option they can hardly exercise.

DO NOT BUY OPTIONS. SALE!

Know that if you want to multiply your money fast, you should risk it by buying Calls or Puts.

But this book is for basic beginners. Here you first want to learn. He wants to survive the market. Do the right thing, safer.

Also, you do not want to buy a stock or option and keep praying to Hail Mary for the market to go up. And you do not even want to sleep with a hot head because you took a loss of 20% of your capital in one day.

There is a theory called "max pain theory" or "Maximum Pain Theory".

It indicates that statistically, whether by manipulation or at The Chance of God, the price of assets on the eve of maturity will position itself exactly in the value that will generate the maximum of "pain" in reais for the holders of options. That is, it is the price where most of the options will generate dust.

Whether by manipulation or by market coincidence, in this book the suggestion is that you do not buy options. Just bid options. Most of them will turn to dust. Do not have them!

But only sell as I explain below.

AN INTERESTING STRATEGY

Now, I am going to show you a remarkably interesting strategy for operating options.

There are dozens, if not hundreds of options strategies. There are award-winning books just talking about them.

Here because it is a beginner's manual, let us focus on a conservative and profitable strategy.

If you simulate it in the opções.net.br see that there is no type defined for it.

This is because the strategy demands the use of fundamentalist analysis to filter the assets.

The other options strategies out there are speculative, and so the fundamentals of the assets you are operating are indifferent. Therefore, the other structured strategies have the bias of valuing the option for later resale and with this to earn the profit.

Already here in our strategy, the goal is to receive monthly fixed income, maintain the possibility of performing swing trade, and at worst, to be positioned in a good asset to receive dividends.

Of course, in certain specific assets we can apply the strategy even if the moment of the company is not the best, such as an asset with high equity value and great possibility of recovery, but that is on its historical floor because of some occasional event, such as Coronavirus.

The strategy is to sell a call well above the current asset price

(OTM, Out of Money) and sell a put well below the price, that is, also OTM.

Below is a fictitious example of what our graphic marking with PETR4 would look like and the release of 1000 CALLS and 1000 PUTS:

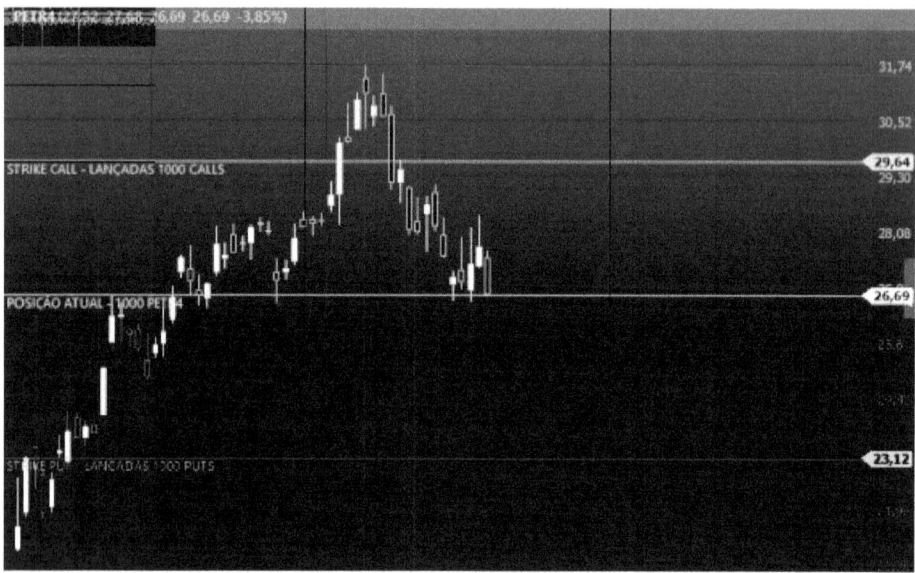

Note that our current position is 1000 PETR4 with an average price of R$ 26,69.

The price of the asset currently is R$ 26,69. We buy the market now. Investment value, R$ 26,690.00. It is 1000 PETR4.

We sell (launch) 1000 CALLS with strike R$ 29.64, for the nearest maturity.

We also sell 1000 PUTS with strike R $ 23.12, for the nearest maturity.

For CALLS, let us say we receive a prize of R$0.29 for each CALL. That is, as there are 1000 CALLS, our prize was R$ 290.00 reais, received at the time of sale.

For THE PUTS, let us say we receive a prize of R$0.23 for each PUT. As there were 1000 PUTS that we launched, we received R$ 230.00

reais to be seen by them.

OK. The operation is structured. It is mounted.

We are positioned in the asset, and we have two derivatives sold, an OTM call and an OTM put, that is, out of the money.

The strike of the call is approximately 9% above the current price, and the put is approximately 10% of the current price.

For maturity, there are 3 scenarios:

1- If on the day of expiration of these options the asset is in the middle of the strikes, the two will expire, turn to dust, and with that we will have received the award without being exercised.
2- If the asset is above R$ 29.64 on the day of maturity, we will be exercised on the call. The put will turn to dust. We will have received the prizes, and on the day of the year we will receive the sale of the PETR4 share, which will be sold for R$ 29.64, even if the current price is R$ 60.00. That is the risk. But to take that risk, we will have received the award.
3- If on the day of maturity, the asset is below the strike of the put, that is, below R $ 23.12, we will be required to buy PETR4 at the price of R $ 23.12, even if the asset is costing 16.00 in the market. That is the risk.

Now, let us go to the profitability of this operation in each scenario.

Scenario on expiration day	Profitability	Advantage	Disadvantage
Asset Price in the middle of strikes	Profitability 1% per month	Keep the asset in a portfolio and can sell it to the market	The asset may rise in the meantime, but you will not be able to sell it before matur-

		later.	ity. It may fall too, and you will repeat the operation.
Asset Price above call strike	Profitability 1% per month. + sale of assets	Avoid the "hand of lettuce"	"Lose" a good asset in portfolio, which could yield even more.
Asset Price below put strike	Profitability 1% per month	Reduce your Average by 5%	Buy above the current price

1- In scenario 1, we are positioned at 1000 PETR4 that we invested R$ 26,690.00.

By call we received R$ 290.00, which means 1.08% on top of the invested capital.

For the put, we received $ 230.00. If we are exercised in the put, the cost will be R $23,000.00. This is the amount that is reserved in the broker as margin. So, the prize of R$ 230.00 means a return of 1% on top of the margin capital.

On the day of expiration, the options turned to dust, you stayed with your profitability above, and keep your 1000 PETR4 to repeat the operation for this new maturity. If PETR4 is above your purchase price, you can even sell it now if you want to completely terminate the operation and move on to another asset.

What if PETR4 fell? It is all right, I'm not going You will repeat the operation by selling another call and another put.

2- In scenario 2, the profitability of the options will be the same. The difference is that you will still have the profitability of the sale of the asset, as it was exercised in the call. As the call had strike in 29.64 and our average price was 26.69, we will receive in the swing trade, when exercised, the value of R $ 2,950.00 reais.

3- In scenario 3, the least favorable, we received the profitability of the above awards, however, we were exercised at PUT. Our penalty for this will be to reduce our average price by 5%. (Because the put was 10% below our average price). When exercised, you can already repeat the operation for the next month.

Important: You cannot sell your asset before maturity because it is given as a guarantee from CALL. Therefore, if you want to sell the asset, you must repurchase the CALL.

The "hand of lettuce" is the hand that releases (sells) the asset as soon as it sees reaching profit.

To occur the hand of lettuce, you need to repurchase the call. That is where the secret is.

Because when the market sees great expectation of the asset rise (even if you do not even know this expectation), the price of calls is up there, and then you even wanting your hand lettuce, will not lettuce, because it will be expensive to buy back the calls.

So, you will not make the mistake of selling an asset that there is great expectation of going up even higher. You will sell only for the strike you have chosen as satisfactory for your month.

And the last warning: Don't sell PUT assets you do not want to buy in that strike. If you do, you will do what analysts call an "average price" and that is dangerous.

Buying an asset, you already have at a price below your average price is good, if the asset pays dividends or has great growth potential.

If it is a "bad" asset, you should not do this. By the way, you should not even touch him.

Leave it to the speculators. You are an investor.

FINAL CONSIDERATIONS

This work sought to guide you efficiently and intensively to the healthy operation within the financial market.

Your next step now is to seek the most technical literature on the stock market.

There are several books on the subject, several renowned authors, and lots of content for you to delve into.

Do not forget risk management, where you never put more than 15% of your assets into an operation. In the same sector.

I also suggest that you do not "mentor" in which the "analyst" tells you which asset to buy.

TD Ameritrade´s Think or Swim has free 3 research teams information for all stocks updately weekly, so this can be very usefull.

No more, good reading and good investments.

www.ingramcontent.com/pod-product-compliance
Lightning Source LLC
Chambersburg PA
CBHW070811220526

45466CB00002B/633